NORTHERN DELIGHTS

Best wishes Shirley
from Marilyn
May 2019 xxx

Published in paperback in 2017 by Sixth Element Publishing
on behalf of Marilyn Jordan

Sixth Element Publishing
Arthur Robinson House
13-14 The Green
Billingham TS23 1EU
Tel: 01642 360253
www.6epublishing.net

© Marilyn Jordan 2017

ISBN 978-1-912218-15-8

British Library Cataloguing in Publication Data. A catalogue record for this book is
available from the British Library.

Marilyn Jordan asserts the moral right to be identified as the author of this work.

Printed in Great Britain.

This work is entirely a work of fiction. The names, characters, organisations, places,
events and incidents portrayed are either products of the author's imagination or used in
a fictitious manner. Any resemblance to actual persons, living or dead, or actual events is
purely coincidental.

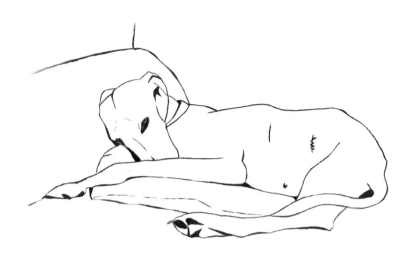

NORTHERN DELIGHTS

A book of illustrated poems
by Marilyn Jordan

With additional illustrations
by Helen Hancox And Lee Hancox

For best results,
read with a fine Middlesbrough accent.

"This remarkable place, the youngest child of England's Enterprise, is an infant, An Infant Hercules."

William Gladstone

NORTHERN TOWN

These northern towns,
always changing, just the same.
This one's different, this one's mine
I hurt when you stumble, I love when you shine.

Northern Powerhouse?
We were the first, we were the best,
standing proud above the rest.
We led the world, we showed the way.

We made bridges, we made ships.
We made iron and steel.
Our 'Transporter', clad anew
Grand Lady of the Tees.

This northern town.
My Infant Hercules,
crossed the world
with giant strides.

This northern town.
This dusty shadow
I hurt when you stumble
I still love when you shine.

GRACIE, QUEEN OF THE SOFA

Greeted at the door, flap of ears, wag of tail.
She stretches languidly,
front, then back.
Her eyes full of happy expectation.

And indeed! She is Gracie Goodgirl!
We are all joy and praise.
With Herculean effort, she has endured.
And slept all day in the sun.

Ah, but yesterday! Her teeth got bored!
Naughty Gracie chewed the rug.
Ate a pen, blue lips grinning nervously
Miss Demeaner, sent to the garden naughty stair.

Evening comes, we watch the news.
Gorgeous Gracie, sprawls supreme.
The Queen of the sofa
has five hours snoring to fit in before bedtime!

ROBIN HOOD'S BAY STATION

I'm no 'train buff', let's be clear,
but they say nostalgia
is always better for keeping.
And Baytown station was a little bit of heaven.

My childish eyes drank it in,
the ticket office, neat and trim.
Ladies' waiting room, freshly painted.
Don't gentlemen ever wait, I wondered?

Red geraniums announced, 'Robin Hood's Bay'
In a prize-winning display.
Every bench and fire bucket,
still marked 'Property of LNER'.

Station Master, hat pushed back,
nods to friends and trippers.
His pipe only removed for
drinking, sleeping and eating.

What a grand way
to start a holiday,
all those years ago.
But how I hated leaving.

If I could see it once more,
as it was, just for a moment.
I'd sit on that bench,
and wave to all the engine drivers.

THE DOG BUS

The Dog Bus, or blue Ford Fiesta,
corners slowly.
Its precious cargo
leans sedately to the left, and straightens up.

Three large doggie passengers
stare thru nose smeared windows,
at other dogs,
passing by, on foot.

Eager to be there,
to walk along that green,
and chase that ball,
all around the park.

Windows now steamed up,
the gang whine gently,
urging their driver into top gear.
Is it still the twenty zone?

Handbrake on. They've arrived!
Exiting Bus with
more enthusiasm than grace,
a bound, and sniff of the air.

The ordeal of a five minute journey
instantly forgotten, distracted
by the unmistakable
'Eau de Squirrel'.

THE PHOTO BOX

There's a place in my house,
I can go there any time,
and in a moment
be transported to the past.

It's not a Tardis, or a time machine,
it's the cupboard under the stairs.
No Sonic Screwdriver,
just a battered cardboard box.

And opening that box,
is an invitation to indulge,
in years and years of snapshots,
the colours of my life.

People, places, special days.
All there, never aging,
I remember every one.
Not a single one anonymous, forgotten.

Childhood friends smile back at me,
visitors and weddings.
Camping trips in soggy fields,
with leaky tents and midges.

The skinny kid with freckles,
smudged by time, becomes my daughter.
Laughing at a different dog,
in a different garden.

The Kodak became digital,
but still I print them all.
Not CD or computer,
my memories, in a box under the stairs.

DANCING SHOES

Slow, slow, quick-quick, and a cha cha cha.
Dancing feet, large and small, dainty clod-hoppers.
Glittery shoes are all around, and
I yearn for such frivolous footwear.

Sparkly, satin, sexy snakeskin.
Ankle straps and dangerous heels.
Sequins, buckles and diamantes,
every colour of my rainbow dreams.

Limp, limp, shuffle, shuffle,
painful feet throb.
My dance shoes, drab and battered,
plainest black, and stumpy heels.

Dance on… ignore the pain.
Waltz, Rumba, Samba, Jive.
If other dancers stare,
they're not admiring the footwork,
just my amazing, orthopaedic galoshes.

My Hobbit feet, in worn out shoes.
Like an ugly sister's,
won't fit in Cinderella's stilettos!
Steel toecaps would be better.

Ruby red, strappy peeptoes!
I want it all, I'll pay the price!
But no! That just won't work. And I go back
to sticking sequins on my slippers!

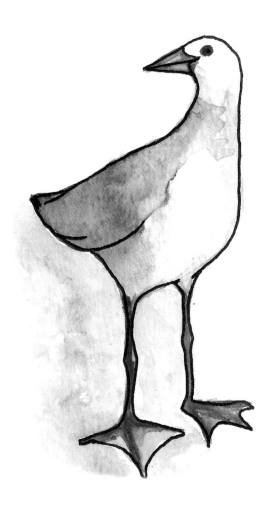

SEAGULLS

Nasty gulls, screeching, squawking, shrill.
Masters of flight,
soaring, swooping overhead.
Messy, thieving scavengers.
I don't like them much.

Snowy white feathers,
pristine, bright.
Cruel, yellow beak.
Glassy, brassy eye.

He'll challenge for your picnic.
Steal your fish and chips.
So many nasty seagulls,
I really don't like them much!

They squawk, and shriek and screech
And
Plop
A
Lot!

But it wouldn't be seaside without them!

WINTER'S BEACH

Winters here are more grey than white,
more damp and grim, than crisp.
Lazy North winds cut right through you,
rather than go round.

A seaside walk,
rarely less than bracing.
Heads down, leaning forward,
eyes slitted against the driven sands.

Winter grey sea,
reflected in a steely sky.
Surf's white horses, rearing, plunging,
racing to the beach.

Angry waves smash,
into the old sea wall.
The stinging spray thrown high.
Watched by a hardy, muffled crowd.

But the beach is never empty,
no matter how grim the day.
Doggy walkers, fresh-air-fiends,
and ever-present joggers.

Once in a while, we get lucky.
No one more surprised than us.
A still, bright day, shocking in its beauty.
The winter sun dazzles,
and Redcar smiles, and breathes again.

SUMMER MORNING

The 5am sunshine creeps
through badly drawn curtains,
it wakes me up too early.
Shouting at my eyelids,
'get up, wake up, rise and shine'.

Like the restless child
unable to sleep,
makes sure that no-one tarries,
lingering, slumbering, abed.

Lured, stumbling, heavy-eyed,
into the garden,
mug of tea in hand.

Birdsong fills the air.
Blackbirds, not yet
worn-out by childcare,
serenade my heart.

Dewy roses, heavy-scented
newly opened with the dawn,
glow with peachy colour,
not yet faded by the day.

Summertime, my time,
I am returned to life.
The sap in my veins
risen again each spring.

HAPPINESS

Who would have believed it?
Not I for one.
I stand before you,
A pensioner!
And declare my happiness.

It comes and goes, for sure,
but never strays too far distant.
Like a steadfast friend,
who turns up fortuitously.

Not enslaved by hormones,
or tyrannical bosses.
The tantruming kids are grown, and
the house seems so much bigger!

Silly things make me smile,
daftness makes me laugh.
A friendly word in a Northern voice,
my stout Yorkshire heart expands.

Regrets? I've had a few,
but then, too few to mention.
Sorry Frank! That just slipped out.
Bad Attitude AND a pension!

Not ruled by restlessness, driven by need.
Still curious now, but calmer.
More appreciative than ever,
of the views along the way.

Life sits easier on my shoulders now,
not weighty or drab.
A many coloured stole,
light as chiffon, warm as sunshine.

FAMILIES

You're in, you're out.
In and out of favour.
Causes unknown or trivial,
to those catastrophic.

Years of not speaking
or heated exchanges.
Words long supressed,
some ought never be released.

Good times were there,
between childish bickering.
Building sandcastles,
then more hurling missiles.

The dirty look, the casual skit.
Precision loaded insults,
perfectly delivered,
from years of target practice.

The Cluster-bomb of accusations,
reverberate for years.
Shrapnel deep embedded,
waiting to resurface.

We grow up, move away.
Distance bringing a veneer
of family feeling, or maybe,
a breathing space, fresh start.

Not really friends, but better relations.
Tentative phone calls,
occasional visits.
Shared memories to laugh at,
carefully avoiding so many elephants in the room!

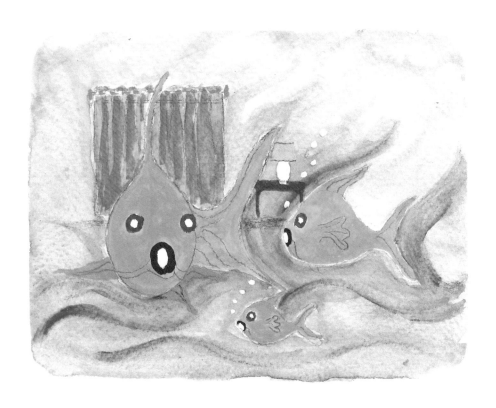

SEA DREAMS

Waking slowly, reluctantly,
half dreaming still.
Soft tendrils of consciousness
clinging to the remnants of sleepy imaginings.

Floating, drifting,
lulled by a warm sea,
lapping around me.
The hot sun on my face.

Briefly, oh so cautiously,
should I take a peep?
Is that the dazzling
blue sky above me?

And the clear Caribbean sea
that holds me
suspended, safely enfolding me,
in its gentling tides.

I long to dive down
through the sparkling waves.
Finning lazily amongst the
jewelled, bright eyed fish.

Damselfish, Blue Tang,
Angel fish and Wrasse,
long shiny Needlefish
and Horse-eyed Jack.

This glittering shoal, tugging at my arms,
tries to draw me back.
Rising slowly, surfacing,
gasping, grateful for air.

Dream filled eyes scan
distant shores searching for my home.
Floating, growing wakeful.
No, let me dream on.

OUT ON THE RAZZ!

Maureen and Brenda are out on the Razz.
Miniskirts, mascara and heels,
they're dressed to the nines,
and raring to go.

The bus into town
marks the start of the fun,
and they head for the Excel Club.

With expectations of romance,
they enter the 'scene'
and survey the available 'talent'.

The resident band is playing,
the girls are eager to dance.
"Tie a yellow ribbon"
soon has them on their feet.

They've seen the Fantastics, the Troggs,
and Mindbenders, Jimmy James and the Vagabonds.
and once, an exotic transvestite dancer.
That was an interesting night!

Tonight's star act is the Drifters,
their all-time favourite group.
"Saturday Night at the Movies",
has everyone singing along.

The lads are now on the dancefloor,
a tap on the shoulder,
an invitation to dance. Not touching,
just moving around the handbags.

A night of dancing and flirting,
dates made,
then the long walk home.
No money left for a taxi.

In just a few hours, breakfast, and
arriving late for work, gritty eyed and clumsy.
Every invoice misfiled, lost for weeks.
The boss says, "Been dancing?"

STUFFED!

I'm so full! Not another
morsel could I eat.
One more chip would finish me
one pea, or lettuce leaf.

No empty corners left, I'm stuffed.
That after dinner mint
would be a step too far.
The outcome could be messy!

I'm stuffed. Did someone make me,
hold a gun to my head,
and say "eat up"?
No. It was totally self-inflicted.

I didn't really eat that much.
My stomach must have shrunk.
I'm sure it was 'Healthy Option'
and I ate less than ALL the others!

Just a starter, and a 'mains',
with a creamy, brandy sauce.
And wedges on the side.
But it was garnished with a salad!

Dessert was heaven-on-a-plate,
Sweet, and tangy and fruity.
Sooo delicious and refreshing
But it wasn't 'Slimmer's World'.

Why do waiters stare, having asked
"Is that with custard, cream or ice cream?"
The answer has to be, "Yes!" and
coffee and liqueurs to follow suit.

I'm so full, it hurts.
Sit up straight, no slouching.
Don't breathe so deep.
Not another morsel could I eat. Ever.

JUST DANCING

Step, step, forward, back,
swaying, moving round the floor.
Hypnotic music, flowing gently,
oblivious to all.

Turning, step, step, back,
close together, heads turned away.
Not talking, just dancing,
swaying gently to the rhythm.

Turning, turning, step, step,
drifting, synchronised.
Turn and counter turn,
spin out, and back.

Forward, forward, turn, back,
the music leads the way.
Long steps gliding forward,
hesitation, turn again.

Side step, forward, turn,
the music swells and flows.
Turn together, dip and sway.
Turning, slowing, music ending, fades away.

MY DARLING GIRL

When you arrived, quite unique,
with orange fluff hair
and jaundiced skin,
the 'just back from Benidorm' look was in.

They pointed out a couple of glitches.
A bump on the forehead,
and wonky toes.
Matron said, "She'll grow out of those."

You slept sometimes, and sometimes not.
We stared at each other,
and shared a few tears, and burpy smiles.
It was scary stuff, you know.

My darling girl, so bright, so clever.
Truly a 'Tuesday's child'.
You've made me laugh, you make me proud.
Always in my heart, never far from mind.

Still unique, kind and caring.
The 'orange fluff hair',
Now glorious gold.
Always, my beautiful, darling girl.